FROM THE COUNTRY OF THUNDER

STEVEN J. WHITE

From the Country of Thunder

GREENSBORO: UNICORN PRESS   1990

"Arizona Five," the monotype on the cover, is a
1984 intaglio, copyright by Arthur Secunda.

Unicorn Foundation gratefully acknowledges support
from The National Endowment for the Arts, a federal
agency, and the North Carolina Arts Council, a state
agency, during the time this book was published.
The publisher wishes to thank Alan Brilliant for de-
signing and handsetting the type (in 12 pt Kennerley)
David Nikias for handprinting the book (on 70-pound
Mohawk Superfine Vellum eggshell finish) and Laurel
Boyd for handbinding this book.

DEDICATION : IN MEMORY OF
MARCELL PALLAIS & TEO SAVORY

Library of Congress Cataloguing-in-Publication Data:
    White, Steven F., 1955-
    From the Country of Thunder.
    I. Title.
    PS3573.H47478B8   1990   811'.54
    ISBN 0-87775-222-2 cloth
    ISBN 0-87775-223-0 paper

UNICORN PRESS, INC.
Post Office Box 3307
Greensboro, North Carolina 27402

TABLE OF CONTENTS

Exalt him that is low,
and abase him that is high.
I will overturn, overturn,
overturn, it: and it shall be
no more, until he come whose
right it is; and I will give
it him.

Ezekiel 21 : 26-27

Υ parece que la vida se ha marchado
hacia el pais del trueno

Joaquín Pasos

ALFONSO

Go to the ant, O sluggard;
consider her ways, and be wise.

Proverbs 6 : 6

His name came to him, but Alfonso
didn't budge. Instead, he finished humming
the song he made up for *los zompopos.*
And an ancient voice from the sun
added the Nahuatl lyrics that only a scattering
of genes in Alfonso's body understood:
tsontli, tsontli poposaktik,
tsontli, tsontli popoa.
An elbow in Alfonso's ribs.
An insult against his mother. Alfonso
shuffled his broken sandals, raising dust
on the way to the window's wooden sill.
'Hurry up!' shouted the overseer, Tomás,
from the shade. 'If *los zompopos*
launch a surprise attack,
this payday will be your last.'
The inkpad was open. Toward it,
Alfonso stretched a dirty hand
mapped with antbites
and the red trails of thorns.
He pressed down his thumb
then left his print
instead of a signature
on a yellow card,
gridded and wrinkled,
which was his book of hours.
'Here! Take your money
and get back to the rosebushes,

3

you slobbering idiot! You're lucky
la señora gave you a job!'
Alfonso smiled, wiped his stained thumb
on the planks of the overseer's house
and began to hum again,
accompanied by the sun.
As he moved through the sweating
crowd of workers,
showing his fistful of money,
someone knocked Alfonso's baseball cap
to the ground. Alfonso picked it up,
put it on sideways the way he wore it,
and continued up the hill toward the big house
and la señora's garden
where lemons and mangos glowed among green leaves
like the eyes of wild animals.
There were other voices now,
a murmuring, as if los zompopos
had heard his song and were joining
the invisible chorus
of all that cannot die.
Alfonso ignored the children
laughing and hurling stones at him.
He remembered how la señora, Doña Eva
had interrupted his dream
of green and yellow parrots
and taken him aside in her garden:
'Alfonso, I know you're good for something.'
And she had given him
a gift worth even more
than the rains
that constellate
the coffee plants with blossoms.

4

'Guard my rosebushes, Alfonso.
Keep them safe from the ants.'
La señora had left him with a bottle
of white powder marked
with a skull and crossbones.
And that was the most horrible
thought of all. How could he kill
los zompopos? Alfonso stopped,
stooped toward a pool of water
beneath a fountain in the garden, brushed
away some fallen petals
to look at his face.
Tsontli, tsontli, whispered the sun.
And Alfonso could imagine
his metamorphosis. The twin tufts
of hair on his balding head—
how much they resembled antennae!
And his jaw seemed more distended.
He felt himself dwindle in the middle
like an hourglass, and energy
pulsed through every fiber of his back.
No. The ants would carry the poison
back to their nest
through all the organs and veins
of Alfonso's new body!

Alfonso was awakened by an owl's cry.
It was dark.
He sensed a tingling in his arms,
legs, stomach, chest, cheek.
The ants had made a highway of Alfonso
and were busy stripping leaves,
everything except the roses,

5

from *la señora's* bushes.
By moonlight, Alfonso
watched the tireless procession
bearing green banners.
He sang.
He tossed his comrades gently into the night,
one by one, knowing they would
regroup and continue their advance.
Soon he felt at peace
in the murmur of the ants.
A little sleep, a little folding
of the hands to rest. And the ants
entered his dreams, carrying
Alfonso away, piece by tiny piece.
He felt no pain.
They were making him whole,
bearing him
on their bodies flowing like sparks
across the vastness of space.

THE FAMILY

Years later, I try to reconstruct
the family, the jasmine
corridors of their mansion
and, outside its high walls topped
with bougainvillaea and jagged glass,
the insurrection.
I imagine them all—
extinct but repeating themselves
with circadian rhythms,
perpetuating the old order, somewhere,
projecting their lives in an absurd film
played continuously for no one.

*   *   *

At dawn, the matriarch, Doña Catalina,
arose from the shrine where she slept,
put on a blue-sequined bathing suit,
unlocked the iron gate
that opened on the patio,
teetered on the edge of eternity
with the first light of day striking
her white swimming cap,
then flopped into the foul water
of the amoeba-shaped pool.
Over the eighty years she had inhabited the planet,
she came to believe in her future beatification.
But lacking a miracle or two, she needed
more time to reach sainthood. And so, she feared
death. Since *el diablo*, one morning,
had grabbed her ankles and almost drowned her,

she swam a shorter lap so as not to disturb
the deeper waters where the scum and dead leaves
of evil accumulated in silence. It was a standoff,
but she counted her blessings. 'How many
people,' Catalina asked her grandson Henri,
'have come from battling *el diablo*
with only a sprained knee?'

*   *   *

The mansion was a single-story labyrinth.
In the country of earthquakes it was best
not to think about the weight of the roof
overhead, but to long for the sky's lightness.
Despite her great powers, Doña Catalina
had been unable to master
the tremors that continued
to shake the foundations of her country.

When the massive gates were pushed open
by a guard with a machine gun slung
across his shoulder, a visitor beheld
an exquisitely fortified paradise.
Watchdogs rested in the shade of a mango tree.
Metal flowers and leaves disguised
the bars covering each window of the mansion.

In the dining room, the somber
portraits on the walls, the massive table,
the white linen, the conspicuous silver handbell
to call the servants, and the leather chairs
blackened by the years
suggested the sensibility of a feudal age.

Doña Catalina gummed two soft-boiled eggs
at the head of the table, and watched her insomniac
daughter-in-law, Eva Dulcevida de Panais,
wander in her silk bathrobe in search of morning coffee.
The two women battled each other
with silence and secret spells.

Of Eva's four children (Henri, Pierre, Solange
and the youngest, Petit Larousse), only Henri
remained in the country. The others
wanted to study abroad forever.

Henri got up at nine o'clock, walked past
his magazines of perfect tits and cunts,
showered, dressed, never bothered with breakfast,
grabbed some fat manila folders,
strolled across the patio to the office,
sat down at his desk beneath a huge
topographical map of the country
and a plaque from his father, François ('Don't
wait to be a great man, be a great boy!'),
then began his daily maneuvers to salvage
his father's disintegrating
farms and businesses.

François never appeared before noon.
Hungover and struggling like his mother
with certain horned demons, he usually ate lunch in bed.
He pushed a button by the air conditioner controls
and the kitchen intercom crackled,
halting the servants' chopping, stirring and
gossiping: 'Tell Fredi to get his ass
up in the lemon tree so I can have a lemonade

with some aspirin when you bring my lunch.
Understood?' François sat up and sank his bulk
into some pillows. If only he could
get a decent night's rest. The bed where he slept
alone behind a steel-reinforced, triple-locked door
was too lumpy. But he wasn't about to remove
his arsenal—the sawed-off shotgun, the Uzi
submachine gun and the 9mm automatic pistol
he kept under his mattress. Ever since
the loaded pistol had fallen, discharged
and blown a hole in the ceiling, the servants
were extremely careful when they made François's bed.

*   *   *

There were weapons throughout the mansion:
under cushions in the living room, in the closet
with the mops and brooms, in an empty sugar bowl
and in a secret tunnel that went
from Eva's room to a hill beyond the outer walls.
The weapons were brought in after the rebels
raided a Christmas party and held François
and his friends for ransom. Henri, meanwhile,
on a mescaline trip in the northern mountains,
floated over a field of strawberries, south
over the Pacific, south toward Easter Island's giant
faces of fallen stone. François,
an expert in the dynamics of rum, and convinced
that the celebration should go on, had tried to kiss
the young woman in olive-green fatigues
who was holding a gun to his neck.
He still had the scar on his forehead
from the blow of her pistol. The blood

had ruined his favorite shirt—a white *guayabera*.
Now, five years later, he was number four
on the list of those who would be shot
for crimes against the people.
François closed his eyes and dreamt of dollars
that refused to float down from the trees he strangled
with fury. The oxidized dinosaurs
of all his unfinished projects collapsed in his brain.
'Where's my goddamn lunch?' he screamed.

*   *   *

Eva was worried. She paced away the afternoon
in her bedroom, thinking about the war and the circles
of fire and the distant shores of night
in another country. She knew the family
would be struck by those who live in lightning.
If only she could sell the mansion and leave.
But the interested buyer refused to pay
vast sums without the blueprints in hand.
And they had disappeared, rolled away
into the color of the sky—just when the sale
seemed certain. Suddenly, Eva realized
that Catalina, the old sorceress, had simply
rendered them invisible so that she
would never be uprooted from her house.
Eva decided to launch a counterattack
while Catalina communed with the shadows at Mass.

If Henri had not gone waterskiing
with the company lawyer in the crater of an old volcano,
he would have seen the strange procession
winding through the mansion's corridors

11

that afternoon. It was not an elaborate
ritual for the extermination of cockroaches.
One of the servants, Carmen, came first,
lifting a crucifix over her head. Eva followed,
head bowed, hands clasping a Bible. Then came
María, another trusted servant, swinging
a metal bowl filled with burning incense.
In unison, they chanted:
'God bless the good, and evil condemn,
just like Jesus in Jerusalem.'
Catalina returned an hour later, understood
the threat at once, and smiled.
Soon she was parading through the house
flinging drops of Holy Water everywhere,
mumbling her effective litanies.
Eva poured herself a drink and wept.

*   *   *

Eva dreaded nights in the mansion.
Catalina would remove her wig, put on a red
silk scarf and a white robe, then inject
her son's buttocks with 'vitamins.' Henri
would go to clandestine meetings
and leave his slalom ski locked in the car.
Jasmine grew through the bars of Eva's window
and filled her bedroom with the smell of freedom.
She drank whiskey from a crystal bottle
and kept putting her hands over her ears—
not to block out the sound of gunfire and explosions
a few kilometers away in the capital, but so
she wouldn't have to listen to François finger
the same ten notes over and over on the piano.

12

She opened and closed and opened the drawer
where her petite derringer nested.
François was slumped over the piano,
his nightly bottle of rum
by his right hand that played the melody of life.
Finally, his head hit the keys,
striking the chord the servants
patiently awaited. They came
into the room and lugged François to bed.

FIRST DAY

The sting of sweat in his eyes. The ring
of the invisible foreman's machete
cutting into the deep patterns
of a landscape that dazzles and
tortures the foreigner with its beauty.
The gringo stops because he finds
he has no language
to express the sound and movement
of a hundred green and yellow parrots
circling the sun. And this sun
ignites in his brain a strange fire,
which spreads until he is aware
that everything is other
and he thrives in it,
though he knows he doesn't
belong there. The gringo
watches in awe as the entire length of the snake
twists like a turbid current
between the row of coffee plants he is picking
and the row given to a better worker
who left him far behind He empties
the basket strapped to his belly and begins
to labor again. But it's hopeless!
Even blind old Carmen, with her one good arm,
picks ten times more coffee than the gringo.
'Who is he and what's he doing here?'
Carlos asks Santo after the foreman
blows the bull's horn
and fires his gun and everyone
has come from shadows
down the steep slope to assemble

for lunch in a clearing.
'I don't know. People say he's the friend
of the *patrón's* son. He must be rich.'
'Why? Because he's a gringo?'
'No. Because his boots are new.'
'How much do you think they cost?'
'I asked him this morning. He said they were cheap—
only thirty dollars.'
'How much is that?'
'A month's wages.'
'Cheap? That son of a bitch couldn't pick enough coffee
during the whole harvest to buy those boots.
Look how little coffee there is in his sack now.
He'd starve here if he had to live on what he earned.'
The pickup rattles to a halt with its load of food—
a wooden crate of tortillas
and two metal motor oil containers
filled with beans and rice. The gringo
stands in line for lunch and wonders
if he can bear what the afternoon will offer.
'Hey,' says Carlos. 'Should we tell him
to cut some banana leaves for his hands?'
'No. He thinks he knows everything.
Let's just see what happens,'
replies Santo as the gringo starts juggling
the steaming tortilla from hand to hand.
And when Juanita spoons out
hot rice and beans on top of the big disk
of corn the workers call 'un long-play,'
the gringo hurries to sit down, shaking
one hand then the other as he tries to balance
the whole sliding business on his knees.

15

'Look,' laughs Santo. 'The gringo's
tortilla split
and the beans
are running
down the crotch
of his new pants.'
'I thought gringos were supposed to be smart.'
'Not this one.'

THE OVERSEER

Closing his eyes, Tomás focuses his pain
and recalls driving toward the city at dawn:

He tightened his grip on the steering wheel
as the pickup bounced over washboard-ruts
made by heavy trucks
bearing cattle, coffee and bananas
from the mountains.
In the back of the pickup,
Juanita, the cook, held the fever-stricken head
of her son Miguelito and rubbed his stomach.
Tomás glanced at his passengers
in the rearview mirror
and then at the empty seat beside him.
The law of gravity kept the pickup
rattling down the potholed road
and there were other laws,
preserving another order,
that explained why Tomás, the overseer,
sat alone behind the wheel
and why the two *campesinos*,
on their way to see a doctor,
were covered with dust in the back.

Tomás opens his eyes and then his hand.
Lying in the hospital bed
and grimacing beneath bandages,
he studies the bullet
the doctor dug from his head.

After five years as overseer,
Tomás wonders if his salary has eroded his past.
But he can still remember a childhood
that resembles Miguelito's:
chopping firewood and hauling endless
buckets of water so his mother
could make tortillas, beans and rice;
hunting iguanas and roasting them
over smoky fires; scrounging among
the coffee plants for the fallen red berries. . .
An image surfaces inside Tomás—a child
wearing no shirt or shoes. The boy smiles
and lifts a dead armadillo in one hand
and a machete in the other.

Was it Tomás or Miguelito with the armadillo?
Miguelito's life was superimposed on Tomás's,
and the child repeated his father's face.
Hadn't Tomás been using Juanita for his pleasure
since his wife refused
to leave the comforts of the city?

Tomás's only visitor wants to see the bullet.
'What happened?' asks Don François,
the fat but invisible
owner of farms and lives, the one who picked
Tomás from poverty because he knew Tomás
would deny his own 'inferior' blood and obey.
'I drove into the city,' replies Tomás,
'to withdraw money for the coffee pickers.
No one had been paid for two months.
There was talk of a strike!

I had to give them something—
even though the price of coffee
was still falling and you told me
not to sell what we'd harvested already.'
And then Tomás tells the rest of his story:

Returning to the farm on the steep road
that wound past hillsides planted
with coffee and bananas, Tomás saw
a vehicle engulfed in flames
ahead on the road. Two men appeared,
pointing a rifle and a pistol
at the pickup. Tomás slowed, rolled
down his window, reached under the seat
for his .38 revolver, fired
three times and hit one of the gunmen.
The other took cover.
Accelerator to the floor.
Fishtailing in the loose dirt.
Sideswiping the burning roadblock.
Intense heat on the left side of his face.
A gunshot behind him.
The blow to the back of his head.
Out of control. Reaching back.
His hand covered with blood.
Driving, somehow driving.
The green world blurred and flickered.

As he leaves, Don François says,
'I'm glad the money is safe.
Too bad about the boy.
You're lucky
your wife and son weren't with you.

19

I sent someone
to give the woman money
for a coffin. Get some rest.
I need you at the farm.'

Tomás closes his fist around the slug.
He remembers the doctor's voice,
echoing in the hospital room:
'This bullet would have killed you
if it hadn't passed through the boy first.'

NICOLASA

Nicolasa clutched her favorite doll
even tighter when she saw the two figures
holding long poles
as she skirted the building
that hummed with machinery.
Paco and a companion
were working late at the holding tank
filled with water and the coffee
from a few days of harvesting.
They stirred the water
to loosen the dirt on the coffee.
A pump was sucking the fruit
through a presser that separated
the pale bean from its red hull.
'You're missing your birthday party, *mamacita!*'
shouted Paco, remembering Nicolasa's tiny breasts
and the way she squirmed under his potbelly
that night on the pile of burlap sacks
while the white beans surged
through a water-filled channel.
'Hey, come back,' said Paco as Nicolasa
passed and continued down the hill.
'What's your hurry?
They'll save some candy for you.'
Light from the building
illuminated her face, disfigured
by the earthquake that wrecked her house
seven years before. Now she was
an orphan with a scar
that resembled a ladder suspended in darkness.
No moon would rise above the mountains.

The drone of insects seemed to warp
and fold the night. An animal dangled
by a rope from a high beam
at the farm's entrance. The party
had begun. Nicolasa took her turn
with the other blindfolded children
wielding a stick. Soon, there was a loud
thwack, like the sound of a rifle butt
striking a stomach. Worthless
coins and candy from the *piñata*
spilled into uplifted hands.

RABIES

While uniformed assassins in jeeps marked *Public Works* patrolled the breathing streets with an antidote to life, the white dog prowled the mountains outside the city and followed the dark river of some slaughter that was flowing in the wind. Here was the great confluence of history.

The cow was sprawled in its blood at Felipe Cruz's feet. It was time to celebrate the end of the coffee harvest. *El Patrón*, Don François, the one without a face, had left word for Felipe to butcher the old infertile cow. The workers would get their traditional chunk of meat.

'It's the least that bastard can do,' thought Felipe, as he flicked his short knife quick as a snake's tongue and removed the whole hide, pulling with his red left hand.

Every week during the four-month harvest either the corn for tortillas or the beans or the rice had run out.

'Someday, *el patrón* will know the knife of fear,' hoped Felipe, kicking the carcass then rolling it from the dirt road onto the hide.

Lino, a coffee picker with a sparse beard, approached Felipe and offered to carry sections of the carcass to a shed nearby where the workers were returning their equipment: the wicker basket for gathering the red berries, the strap to keep the basket snug against the stomach, and the two sacks in which the day's work was dumped and dragged along the rows of coffee plants that snaked across the steep sides of mountains. Felipe pointed and Lino hoisted some ribs onto his shoulder. Blood dripped down his yellow shirt, faded by sweat and riverwashings and sun. Felipe wiped some fat from his knife, pushed his glasses up his nose, then bent over the diminishing cow again. Lino returned with a long-handled axe and spoke softly.

'Felipe, they'll be here tonight.'

'Are they bringing any wounded?' asked Felipe.

'I don't know. But I'm sure they'll be hungry.'

'Save enough meat for them. The best.'

With two strokes of the axe, Lino cracked the spine. A cloud of flies leapt from the bulbous eyes as Lino lifted the cow's head and walked toward the shed.

Felipe paused, stretching his aching back, looked up at the sun that was stealing his air, then down at his work.

'How many will reach the farm tonight?' he wondered. 'Maybe she'll be with them.'

Twelve years ago, Felipe had supplied the rebels before they were exterminated at a secret camp on the hill of the tapirs, Pancasán. The tyrant's troops had swept the countryside, extracting real and invented confessions. Felipe was denounced. Felipe's wife saw the soldiers coming. They shot her as she fled. Then they stripped Felipe, hung him by his thumbs from the branches of a tree, tortured him with knives and left him to die in the same yellow blaze that was ravaging his brain now. But the nightmare itself was emanating from the red mess where Felipe knelt.

Lifting his spinning head from the carcass, sick to his stomach, it was then that Felipe saw the white dog, motionless on the road, snarling with jaws locked in a hideous grin, its saliva dotting the dust.

'Careful,' said Felipe, as he and Lino gathered rocks. 'That dog has rabies.'

They hurled many stones before the dog, inching toward the carcass, finally turned and trotted toward the mountains. Felipe shook his head, took a deep breath, and went back to work, intent on cutting the meat cleanly from the bone.

Now it was dark, and cooler at last. Felipe lit the kerosene lantern in the shed and cleaned the last blood and fat from the windowsill where the workers had lined up for their meat. Some had put their ration in old plastic bags. Others had tied pieces of string around their little bundles of flesh, dangling them over their shoulders the way schoolchildren carry books.

Felipe watched the workers packing their belongings, ready to leave for unemployment in the city or for a patch of land lost in the mountains. How did they manage to survive until the harvest each November? Someone staggered in the moonlight, dead drunk and singing pieces of a melancholy song. A bottle smashed. The figure fell on the side of the road. Considering the immense night sky and the stars, Felipe could not weep for himself or even for others. Soon the tumbling wind would bring the first rains to the dry plants hoarding their blossoms and with them, perhaps, his only child.

Then he heard the growling. There, in a clearing, was the white dog. Felipe took three steps to the far wall where his birdhunting rifle hung from two nails. He loaded the gun, went to the doorway, but couldn't see the dog. More growling. Over there! By the watering trough, the white dog snapped at the air and drooled. Felipe set the lantern on the sill, raised the gun to his shoulder and fired. The shot toppled the white dog, but it rose like a phantom and moved toward him slowly. Felipe pulled back the bolt and a shell hopped into dew-covered grass. As he fumbled for another cartridge, a burst of machine-gun fire ripped the darkness behind him. Felipe dropped to his stomach and saw the dog blown backwards into shadows. When Felipe turned, there were two black boots by his head. He looked up. Fatigues. A smoking muzzle.

'Out hunting again, father? If you're going after big game, you need one of these,' said the young woman, kneeling and patting her weapon.

Felipe embraced his daughter in silence, held her as if she were his last hope, held her and smelled the smoke and the jungle in her hair, held her and wouldn't let go.

'My companions are waiting for me. I'd better leave,' she said, stroking Felipe's face.

As she stood up, Lino stepped into the lantern's light, smiling and carrying a knapsack, a red and black kerchief around his neck.

'Luz María,' said Felipe, certain that a father's ridiculous words Be careful, or Take care of yourself or Good luck were about to cross his lips. 'Remember the saying about the tyrant: Once the dog is dead, no more rabies.'

AFTER THE HARVEST

Bent low, their machetes singing
parallel to the choked earth.
How many fistfuls do they slash
in a day? In a lifetime?

With that sharpened limb
ringing, they clean around
the coffee plants as if each trunk
were a loved one's neck.

I learned to know the nomads
of this crucial,
homeless army
by their hands.

Throughout the countryside,
lost among the weeds,
their severed fingers began
to set down roots.

SOLVING A PROBLEM

What to do with that nasty pulp
from the fruit of the coffee plant?
The piles rise and rot in the tropical sun
because more and more of us
crave those beans.
The pulp pollutes the streams
the way coffee contaminates
our veins. Too acidic
to fertilize the land, what to do,
what to do?
Why not feed it to the cows, ¡Sí!
Feed it to the cows
so they'll feel like swaying their rumps
to Caribbean rhythms—
cumbia, salsa, mambo—
night and day
and the caffeine might raise their I.Q., too,
and a bovine leader could lift a heavy
head and say,
'Let's not be hamburgers
for people in the U.S.A.'
Instead of bulldozing rainforests
for more grazing land,
shovel that pulp
and feed it to the cows
so they can dance and start an insurrection.

DOUBLEHEADER IN PARADISE

So we grabbed the cracked bat
and our four worn-out mitts,
climbed into the old pickup
and began the drive to El Paraíso.

Behind the wheel: Virgilio Pérez, accountant,
resplendent in his full Angels uniform and cleats.
The rest of the team wore tattered caps, torn jeans,
patched shirts and sandals made from tires.

On Sundays, no discussions about class
struggle, or the New Man,
or the revolutionary transformation
of society. On Sundays,

the only ideology was baseball,
a legacy of the foreign troops
that occupied the country
fifty years ago.

And there we were, late for a doubleheader
with the best team in the league.
On the hard road to Paradise,
we got a flat tire,

but there were so many potholes
that we didn't even know it
until the wheel was dented
almost beyond repair.

With a coat of dust on our heads,
we resembled a team of ancient ballplayers,

dragged from retirement on a Sunday
hot enough to stop a weak heart.

Then the wooden sides of the pickup snapped
on a curve, spilling part of the team
onto rocks that fractured bones
and tore flesh from faces.

Not even a winning season
would have made this journey
toward Paradise any easier.
The wayfarers needed inspiration.

What if Dante Alighieri
was sitting in my place, next to
Virgilio, the driver? Would God have shouted,
'Play ball!' in *The Divine Comedy*?

And when Dante waited for the big pitch,
ready to square the sacred circle,
would God have thrown a beanball
so the poet could see the other stars?

I entertained this ridiculous notion
until Virgilio somehow got himself
and the rest of us
to Paradise. What a privilege

to be there! During both games,
I felt almost enlightened—
even when it was my turn at bat
and, as usual, I struck out.

THE RING OF CHILDREN

The truck rumbled into the heart of the future
as Chico downshifted and swerved around deep potholes.
His past was the cloud of dust behind the truck,
the heat waves rising in the afternoon sun.
He wanted to be the single spark
igniting the sacred horror of the blaze
that resolves antinomies in pure energy.

Chico imagined himself appearing
on the city's walls with the other martyrs.
Immortality in the hands of a child
roaming midnight streets with bucket and brush,
resurrection in the hiss of spray paint.
But Chico's dream of one falling body
triggering another and another without end
had inoculated him against death.

Chico heard his comrades
load their weapons,
move stacks of cinder blocks
in the back of the covered truck and adjust
pulleys that raised the outside canvas flaps.
It was simple. They were going to drive
into the garrison and open fire.

The surface of what happened to Chico was destroyed.
Bullets smashed the windshield.
Reality was the galaxy of glass
suspended before Chico's eyes.

He may have slid from the truck
when a bullet hit his right shoulder
and the world flashed white.
He may have been crawling
toward some strange horizon
where schoolchildren streamed at him
like meteors.

And the figure in a black cassock embracing him?
The ring of children enclosing
them both, and moving with them?
The stone steps they climbed?
The cool sanctuary of the cathedral?

UNPREPARED

They wanted to experiment
with a more manageable war
before launching the project for Global Peace.
So, fifty meditators flew south
with their mantras and their guru,
and booked some suites
in a tiny republic's best hotel.
They had faith. They were ready
to transmit the miracle
that would halt the insurrection.
But when they closed
their eyes in formation, the energy
began flowing the wrong way!
What wavelength was this?
They were unprepared
for giant sea turtles
that swam under the surface of their skin
or freshwater sharks
circling behind their eyes
in a great lake of light;
unprepared for the multitude
of trees and plants they couldn't name,
that began to sprout from their scalps;
unprepared for the guerrillas
lying in ambush in their hair;
unprepared for the stinging ants
teeming over their torsos;
unprepared for the lava
bubbling in their brains

and the smell of sulfur
from the center of the earth
that burned their nostrils;
unprepared for the aerial bombardment
of their system and the soldier who laughed
while bayoneting their newborn dream of peace.
As the meditators ran for their lives,
tanks came crashing
through their rib cages
and bursts of gunfire
creased their hearts.

REVERIE ON THE BUS

Green sabers, the banana trees. Scarlet macaws
cruising toward the volcano's sulfuric plume.
Someone opens the window of the packed bus
to escape into the landscape,
to free his mind
from the savagery that has permeated
the most mundane acts of life.
A passenger just jumped from the back door
into hot sunlight and dust
without paying. When the teenager
who was helping the driver collect fares
chased after him, the passenger
lunged with an unpardonable knife
and almost slashed the kid's throat.
Someone wonders: How can this be?
What times are these?
Someone thinks: After the war, people
will create themselves,
construct the things of life, learn to explore
the possibilities of the future tense.
The man who has killed will say: *These are the eyes.*
This is the table. The woman
who has killed will say: *These are the hands.*
This is the mango on the table.
They will touch each others' hands, eyes,
face, chest and sex
with a kind of desire
linked to survival in a different way
because gunfire, explosions

and the moaning of the wounded
no longer will be mixed with the cries of love.
Their experience will nourish
their innocence. *This is the tortilla,
the rice*, they will say. *These are the beans.*
If the objects that have lost
their names in the conflict
forgive and decide not to revolt,
not to punish, not to
crush the faces
of men and women,
the man and the woman who have killed will say:
This is the plow. These are the seeds.
This is the earth and the water.
And they will converse with the sky.
The corn sprouts into a fresh verb: stalks.
The ears form. Tassel.
Shape sunlight into kernels.
It will be the harvest
of a new form of speech.
Words will embrace each other
like the arms of rivers
consoling the beloved that lie in unmarked graves,
rejoicing in their descent through healing fields
and faces, weeping with pure joy
when they see the smokeless skies
and the cities bathed in sunlight
finally at peace.
After the war, someone whispers, *after the war.*
The bus has stopped and someone
feels a metallic object

pressing against the back of his head,
draining the light from his reverie.
It is the barrel of a machine gun.
A voice says: *This is the subversive.*
Get off the bus.
Someone gets off the bus.
Releasing the safety of the weapon,
the man who will kill says:
Put your hands against the bus.
Someone puts his hands against the bus.
But the metal is too hot to touch.

ASSASSIN FOR HIRE

Death to lasers!
Death to long range missiles!
Death to rifles that kill at 1000 meters!

He would close the gap between the warring pairs
of eyes, ears, lungs, hands and feet.
Here is a man who loathes distance.

He prefers weapons with an edge.
I can cut a man's throat, crush his larynx and break
his neck without a sound before he hits the ground.

Now he is on the tyrant's payroll.
He trains troops who do not speak his language.
His mustache looks peculiar. He drives an orange jeep.

He believes he is invincible.
Laws for him are rumors, matters of opinion.
He is employed, and the market can't be wrong.

There is no chance for combat in his own country.
Here, he bores through the enemy he craves
and says he serves this tyrant to serve his nation.

But he is thousands of years old, a member
of the warrior class whose eyes pierce
a darkness that is always feudal.

His body matches the night—black uniform,
black headmask, black fingerless gloves.
He breathes and moves with his target.

He strikes! The blade flashes!
Love is a sentry he removes with ease
to infiltrate the psyche.

THE WHITE HAND

Round twelve. Armando watches the famous boxer
from his country block an opponent's jab
then blast him senseless
with a left hook. The spectators with Armando
in the restaurant shout
and embrace, knocking over tall glasses
of tamarind juice and vodka. Everyone
but Armando cheers the image of the national hero
that circles the planet through networks
of wires and filaments as a pulse of energy
rebounding from a satellite.
'—has beaten nearly fifty opponents
to become the world champion today here in—'
One for each year the tyrant and his family
have been in power, thinks Armando, who realizes
that no one else is listening to the television.
He touches the deep cut on his forehead.
Winners and losers. Armando had considered the odds
of an insurrection in his country, then
bet his life on it. And here
a life is worth nothing—especially if someone discovers
that Armando staged yesterday's robbery
against himself to finance the rebels. He recalls
how the nameless guerrilla
tied him to a chair in the office
with knots as unyielding as his line of thought,
knots that stop circulation. As he stuffed
Armando's cash into a sack, he said,
'Compañero, all the corruption has made business

impossible for you, an honest capitalist. We'll remember
your collaboration. After the triumph, you can
keep some of your farms and factories. Free fatherland—'
'—or death,' replied Armando.
He gagged Armando then suddenly struck him with his pistol:
'Your story will be easier
to tell with a little blood.'

In the restaurant, Armando
wonders how long his role
will remain anonymous in a country
where certain secrets swallow other secrets
until everything is known about nothing.
Two young men with shaved heads begin staring
and pointing at Armando
from a nearby table. One stands up, turns
to the waitress and shouts,
'Hey, you! Bring me a plate of fried testicles!'
The place falls silent. People hurry to leave.
La mano blanca: the death squad's polar flower
opening and closing like a fist in the tropical night.
'Yeah,' says the other. 'And I want a baked arm!'
The waitress trembles, but stands still.
'Forget it,' says the one who spoke first.
'Let's go,' says the other as they walk
directly to Armando's table. Their pistols,
tucked in their belts, bulge like hard-ons.
'Something stinks in here, doesn't it, pal?'
says one, slapping Armando on the back.
The other bends over and pulls Armando's ear
toward a whisper. Then both of them are gone.
Armando stares at his expensive watch.

41

The White Hand.
In twenty-four hours,
who will be able to recognize
his body?

THE FLOWERS

I returned to the city of fire, where the walls spoke
of burying the enemy's heart in the mountains,
where the sniper's ghost
stood in the charred socket of a window.
Then the men in the jeep
drove into my dream
watching rooftops with their weapons poised
and continuing through the new order
of rubble and streets torn up
to make barricades.
They stopped at the house of the flowers.
Two men remained with the jeep
and pissed on the wheels in moonlight.
Three others entered a doorway.
The music stopped and they stepped
into an incendiary silence.
The men who had spent their last coins on rum
walked among the flowers and pointed
with their rifles.
In three little rooms with cardboard walls,
Rosa and Violeta and La Cachimba
stripped and spread their legs.

FOR THE ANNIVERSARY OF HIS DEATH

Each year
The last fires
Do not wave to him
When he passes that day
Because he is fire
In the rifles of those who bear
His name
Who have seen his word
Not his silence
Set out like starlight or astral wind
Tireless guide in the mountains
Of night

Then he still
Finds himself in death
As in the living fabric
Of his followers
He is not surprised
At the earth
And the love of a woman named Blanca
And the shamelessness of the tyrant
As today the twenty-first of February
Feeling the first rains against his gray Stetson
Hearing the bullets sing and the falling begin
And bowing his head to no one

THE GHOST ON THE RIVER

The old man held a book open
to the closing circle of years.
He was sitting in a blue rocker by the river,
resisting the current of his memory.
Was it more dangerous for him
to remember or to forget?
Which was worse—forgetting
what he had done, or remembering
having done something he never did?

The old man wandered the unlit passages
of these questions. He was terrified
as he lifted his eyes from the yellow,
insect-tunnelled pages
he had written decades before.
The ghost rose from the river.
Took form. Remained transparent
to the jungle's green dreams.
But, no, it was not the ghost of the tyrant
that the old man had helped ascend to power
when he was young and believed
a strong hand should shape the world.

Nor was it necessarily
a projection of the old man
imagining how he would soon relinquish his atoms
to the river that disintegrates
personal history and bears the other
dead travelers: adventurers, contrabandists,
speculators in land, lumber, bananas and cattle,

evangelists, hunters of sharks and wild animals,
exporters of monkeys and parrots,
botanists, and engineers who dreamed
of this throat of land and the glory
and fortune of cutting a canal between oceans.

Who, then, was this ghost rising from the river?
The rapid transit of years
had washed away some names
from the banks of the old man's brain.
But he remembered that the ghost
had known fame in life
as the author of a novel
about a boy and a raft
on another river, and that
the ghost had floated past
this very place a hundred years before.
'Mark Twain,' muttered the old man.
'When he came down this river
on his way from San Francisco to New York,
my mother still hadn't been born,
and this farm didn't exist.'
The pages of the book in the old man's lap
turned in the breeze. He had written about Twain,
using passages from the letters
Twain had drafted during his trip across the isthmus:
'gleaming cataracts of vines pouring sheer down
a hundred and fifty feet—wonderful waterfalls
of green leaves as deftly overlapping each other
as the scales of a fish.' He admired Twain
for having taken particles from rivers
to create not the author's face

but the features of a whole culture
that the old man had spent a lifetime
worshiping above his own.

There were other phantoms moving
toward the old man now,
abandoning the mist of the river,
floating over the fields
toward the farmhouse,
the veranda, the blue rocker
where he contemplated
his good intentions, his false memories
and the insurrection that refused to die
while the tyrant's son remained in power.

The new spirits
that the old man could no longer
exclude from his reverie stood before him—
seven weaponless guerrillas.
They were half-naked and hungry,
soaked by rain and river,
delirious, torn by thorns,
and wounded by gunfire.
After the surprise attack on the barracks,
they had eluded
the tyrant's troops and helicopters
for three days and three nights.
These men and women had survived,
and they were seeking refuge
in the old man's final
vision of history.

ELENA ON THE LAKE

Blue and white boats bob on water.
I dip my hand in a mirror.
Drifting alone,
the water the color of the sky.
Children playing onshore,
a baby crying, but then
only the sound of the breeze.
The green poems of God,
these islands with their papayas,
bananas and cocoa trees. Ducks dive
for the same fish that breathe the sea
of Galilee. A heron balances
on stilt-legs in a marsh.

Father Ernesto says our people
who fish these waters
could have been disciples. I have closed
my eyes and seen a man
stand in a boat
to address a crowd on a beach:
'How many of you have fished all night
and caught nothing
because your nets were twisted?'

We eat rice and beans
and fish steamed in leaves.
I help my father sort the fish,
the way we are all sorted by another hand.
No one eats the *moga*. It tastes
like dirt because that's all it eats.

And the *cartilla* is just sharp bones.
But the *guapote, mojarra* and *robalo*
must be the food of our next life—the one
we have glimpsed like the fish
that leap from their world into ours
and try to swim toward the sun.

My brother died at dawn
in the attack on the barracks at San Carlos.
The night before, I had taken him in this boat
to rendezvous
with the others from the islands.
I drifted on the lake until daybreak,
watched the stars disappear
and the birds reappear. I had almost
fallen asleep when the explosions
and the rattle of machine guns began.

The first time I saw my brother
after he had left us, he was walking on the shore.
I had been crying on the lake. The early
morning fog was lifting, and I couldn't
see the figure very well. But when he called
my name, I knew who it was. I took the oars
and rowed quietly through the mist.
The boat scraped sand. I got out.
Warm water covered my bare feet.
Smoke from a fire, fish cooking
over hot coals. 'I've fixed
some breakfast for you,' he said.
And he offered me bread and fish.
I was afraid that if I spoke to him

or tried to touch him
he would leave, and he was gone
when I looked up from my meal.

The lake makes me think. Or
thinks for me. It's late.
I should be getting back.
Soon, but not now.
There's still some light.
And I'm floating through the sky.

THE DIALOGUE

Neither the soldier with Creon's stone face
nor the woman who cannot know
she sees the world through Antigone's eyes
realize that someone in the shadow
of a ceiba tree overhears their words:

SOLDIER: Aren't you ashamed to be asking
about a revolutionary?
WOMAN: Why should I be ashamed? He's my brother,
not a delinquent. You think you go
with God in your hands,
carrying that rifle.
SOLDIER: It's a good thing for you this time
that you're a woman—because this rifle
doesn't bear witness to my anger.
WOMAN: Destroy me then!
The same way you destroyed my brother!

And the listener, protected
by the sacred tree,
watches the wind open
the world
and jumble its human
millennia.

REJECTS

I should send them packing into the void
without a leg to stand on, bury those
pages from an abandoned folder, throw them
into the molten core of that country at war!

Why can't I let my failures go?
Because, like children, they remind me of myself?
Why cannibalize them now?
Their language is stilted, unclear.

Whose ear auscultates this hollow kingdom
where war rumbles skyward to light the land?
It is mine. The time had already come
for me to grasp the outstretched granite hand.

And there were lines about living
on an apocalyptic ledge, my alliance
with a time whose wheels of war turned
in the heart of my adrenaline nights.

Do these fragments possess power
beyond what I consider whole and finished?
The poor bells of the flesh lament these days,
lightless though spired with fire.

How can I sift through my own history
when I remember the retreating guerrillas who burned
their dead comrades' faces to save families from reprisals?
Charred arms embrace the air.

The fragments conjure the tyrant's soldiers retaking
the city, lining up the inhabitants, executing
all those they found with scraped elbows or knees,
and the hospital's director, and even the wounded.

Nevertheless, even though I can smell
the smoke pouring from bombed houses
in the gutted pages, the rejects deserve oblivion.
I'm ashamed of what they say,

even though I accept their selfishness as my own
true face in that rare, transcendent flash of history.
Victory was *a perfect disk of flame framed by my years,*
awakening in me a chiming town at last.

Perhaps, despite years of revision
and many defeated words, I've finally succeeded
in retreating from the hard line of myself
into harder lines that portray other lives.

EPILOGUE

Where did it all happen?

Like lives in a spiral
of past and future, one country relinquishes
its name in these pages as well as a language
in which *death* and *luck* and *strong*
are perfect rhymes.

What if the war there, or here, is truly over?

Peace could be the row of cheap coffins
that gradually fill with hunger.
And there is no truce for the orphans
who sell themselves on city streets
or for the refugees scaling
the throats of foreign systems.
While veterans with the eyes
of frightened animals
try to claw
the violence from their being,
oblivion sings in silent
trenches with the birds
that finally returned.

BOOKS BY STEVEN F. WHITE

POETRY

Burning the Old Year (Unicorn, 1984)
For the Unborn (Unicorn, 1986)
From the Country of Thunder (Unicorn, 1990)

PROSE

Culture & Politics in Nicaragua (Lumen, 1986)

TRANSLATIONS

Poets of Nicaragua: 1918-1979 (Unicorn, 1982)
Poets of Chile: 1965-1985 (Unicorn, 1986)
The Birth of the Sun: Selected Poems of Pablo Antonio Cuadra
1935-1985 (Unicorn, 1988)
Poet in New York (with Greg Simon) (Farrar, Straus, & Giroux, 1988)
From Eve's Rib: Selected Poems of Gioconda Belli (Curbstone, 1989)

ABOUT THE AUTHOR

Steven F. White was born in Abington, Pennsylvania in 1955 and was raised in Glencoe, Illinois. He was educated at Williams College and the University of Oregon. He has traveled and worked in many Latin American countries, including Nicaragua in 1979. He received a Fulbright grant in 1983 to translate poetry in Chile as well as a National Endowment for the Arts Translators Grant in 1988. He lives with his wife and son in Canton, New York, where he teaches at St. Lawrence University.

This is the third volume of his poetry from Unicorn Press, which also has published *Burning the Old Year* and *For the Unborn*, in addition to the bilingual anthologies *Poets of Nicaragua: 1918-1979*, *Poets of Chile: 1965-1985*, and *The Birth of the Sun: Selected Poems of Pablo Antonio Cuadra 1935-1985*. Lumen Books brought out *Culture & Politics in Nicaragua*. His new translation (with Greg Simon) of Federico García Lorca's *Poet in New York* was recently published by Farrar, Straus & Giroux.